*S*equoia and Kings Canyon National Parks embrace some of the most rugged landscapes on earth. Yet there are tranquil places too.
Places where you can find refuge from the concrete and chrome of our present-day civilization. The twin parks of the southern Sierra are yours to explore, to enjoy and perhaps most importantly, to preserve for future generations.

*Several thousand years old,
the oldest giant sequoias seem
rooted in time and stand in mute
testimony to our own puny
three score and ten.*

*Sequoia National Park, located in California's southern Sierra Nevada, was established
in 1890 to preserve giant sequoias and the surrounding forest.
The adjacent **Kings Canyon National Park** was established in 1940 to protect the High Sierra.*

Edited by Cheri C. Madison.
Book design by K. C. DenDooven.

Fourth Printing, 1997

in pictures SEQUOIA & KINGS CANYON The Continuing Story
© 1990 KC PUBLICATIONS, INC.

*"The Story Behind the Scenery"; "in pictures... The Continuing Story";
the parallelogram forms and colors within are registered
in the U.S. Patent and Trademark Office.*

LC 90-60039. ISBN 0-88714-049-1.

*Front cover: The General Grant Tree, photo by
Chuck Place. Inside front cover: Upper Dusy Basin
in Kings Canyon, photo by Pat O'Hara. Page 1:
Moro Rock, photo by Jeff Gnass. Pages 2/3: Sequoia
grove, photo by Ed Cooper. Pages 4/5: Afternoon
reflections at Rae Lakes, photo by Jeff Gnass.*

*in pictures*

# Sequoia
# & Kings Canyon
## The Continuing Story

by John J. Palmer

For 38 years, John J. Palmer wore the green and gray uniform of the National Park Service. He served in 8 national parks, including 18 years as Chief Park Naturalist for Sequoia and Kings Canyon National Parks. He is now on the board of the Sequoia Natural History Association.

CARR CLIFTON

*National park areas are special landscapes set aside by acts of Congress to protect and preserve features of national significance that are generally categorized as scenic, scientific, historical, and recreational.*

*As Americans, we are joint caretakers of these unique places, and we gladly share them with visitors from around the world.*

In September 1890, Congress established Sequoia National Park. One week later, a second law tripled the size of Sequoia and created General Grant National Park. In 1940, General Grant became part of newly-created Kings Canyon National Park. Each park was created to protect and preserve the giant sequoias and the "gentle wilderness" in which they live. Hundreds of canyons, thousands of lakes, and miles of cool green forests support an amazing variety of plants and animals. The parks also serve as places of refuge for man, islands of rest and recreation. So come, inhale the crisp mountain air and savor the fragrant forests. Experience for yourself the tonic of wilderness.

*Mineral King is the jumping-off point for visitors to the high Sierra backcountry.*

# Where the Big Trees Thrive

Colossal trees populate the mixed conifer forests of the southern Sierra Nevada. They reach their climax in the watersheds of the Kings and Kaweah rivers. Here, on unglaciated plateaus at elevations of 6,500 feet, grow forests of giants. Four of the five largest giant sequoias live in this region. While other trees—sugar pine, white fir, and red fir—also reach mammoth size here, they seem insignificant standing beside the true giants. The key to the growth of the super trees is their environment.

Plenty of water, an average of 45 inches a year, and mineral soil ensure sustained, rapid growth. Of course, national park protection means these trees have no fear of the lumberman's axe or the developer's bulldozer. Nature alone determines their fate. How big will they grow? No one knows. The General Sherman Tree is estimated to be between 2,300 and 2,700 years old and still adds about 50 cubic feet of wood to its massive bulk every year.

LARRY ULRICH

◀ *The cinnamon-red, deeply-furrowed trunks of the giant sequoia contrast vividly with the grayish-black, lichen-covered trunks of the white fir. The yellow lichen, called staghorn or wolf, is found on trees throughout the forests but does not usually grow on the giant sequoia.*

*Mature giant* ▷ *sequoias weigh as much as 1,000 tons and reach heights of 270 feet but have no tap root. Instead, they balance their great weight on a shallow root system that penetrates the earth to depths of no more than 5 feet and may spread out over an acre.*

## Misty Moods All Year Long

◄ **Clothing the** feet of the giant sequoias, the brake or braken fern signals the end of summer as its color changes from green to gold. For several months, only infrequent summer thunderstorms dampened the giant trees. Now fog and mist return to the sequoias' realm and the welcome rains of fall begin. As temperatures drop, precipitation increases. The first snows drape the high peaks with a glistening blanket of white. Winter is near.

DAVID MUENCH

▲ *The heavy snows of the southern Sierra, averaging 200-300 inches per year above* *6,000 feet, ensure plenty of moisture for the giant sequoias. Piling up to depths of 10 feet and more, the snow replenishes the groundwater supplies upon which the giant sequoias depend during the rainless summer months. Although sequoias are designed to withstand heavy snow loads, they sometimes fall prey to an extra heavy burden. However, in most instances, other factors also contribute to their downfall.*

# The Forces of Nature That Create Sequoias

LARRY BURTON

◀ **Giant sequoias grow only from seed.** *The chickaree or Douglas tree squirrel plays an important role in the release and dispersal of the seed. Unlike his northern brethren, who eat the seeds of pine and fir, the sequoian chickaree eats only the soft tissue of the green sequoia cone scales. Whether eating cones from the top of a tree or from a cache on the ground, the chickaree scatters the seeds, making them available for germination.*

GERRY REYNOLDS

◀ **Giant sequoias evolved** *with fire. Fire prepares a seedbed by exposing mineral soil. It also sterilizes the soil and creates openings in the forest so sunlight can reach the seedlings. Finally, fire reduces competition from other vegetation, giving the young giant sequoia a head start in life. Without it, the species would cease to exist.*

GERRY REYNOLDS

▲ **No bigger than a** *chicken's egg, the cone of a giant sequoia conceals about 200 tiny seeds, each weighing only 1/5800 of an ounce.*

WAYNE LYNCH—DRK PHOTO

***T**his young sequoia is a* ▲ *survivor. Its companions died from lack of water, overcrowding, or too little sun. With an adequate supply of soil moisture and little competition, it should grow rapidly, reaching heights of 80 to 100 feet in 100 years.*

◀ ***F**ire burned this grove of giant sequoias in 1978. Today, a new forest of sequoias covers the ashes of the old. Some natural thinning has already occurred, but more will be necessary to relieve the severe overcrowding. At best, only a few will survive to maturity.*

# Giants Also Fall

◀ **Wrapped in a** fresh covering of newly fallen snow, the General Grant tree illustrates the beauty of the sequoia forest in winter. The tree is located in Grant Grove, Kings Canyon National Park, and was designated the "Nation's Christmas Tree" by Congress in 1926. Each year citizens hold special Christmas services at its base. Thirty years after President Coolidge honored the tree, it received a second honor. Fleet Admiral Chester W. Nimitz, hero of the Pacific in World War II, visited the park. In accordance with an act of Congress, he proclaimed the Nation's Christmas Tree to be a national shrine in perpetual memory of the country's war dead.

JOSEF MUENCH

*T*his huge giant sequoia limb, ▷ as big as a mid-sized tree, rests on the snow that caused its collapse. Note the contrast between the red heartwood and the white sapwood. As the tree grows in diameter, the wood of the innermost section of the trunk changes to red in color. The chemicals which cause the color make the wood durable.

▼ **The soft, brittle wood of a** mature sequoia causes it to break across the grain when it falls. This brittle characteristic was probably the sequoias' salvation. Initially, loggers considered these monarchs of the forest a prime source for lumber. However, felling the trees did not prove profitable because of breakage. Nearly 75 percent of each giant tree was wasted. Today, most giant sequoias are protected by state or federal law.

CHUCK PLACE

LARRY ULRICH

JOSEF MUENCH

RAY ATKESON

LARRY ULRICH

▲ *The deeply-furrowed, reddish* bark of the incense cedar is often mistaken for that of the giant sequoia. However, its flat, frond-shaped foliage contrasts sharply with the awl-shaped leaves of the giant sequoia.

◁ *The California black oak* (Quercus kelloggii), is the only large deciduous member of the mixed conifer forest community. Growing to heights of 150 feet and only on drier soils, its acorns were prized as food by the Indians.

◁ *The greenish-* white flowers surrounded by four large, white bracts of the Pacific dogwood herald the arrival of spring. You can find its cousin, the creek dogwood, identified by its reddish twigs, along streambeds and other moist sites.

# Variety of Trees

ED COOPER

▲ **In the riot of color that bursts each spring in the**
Sierra foothills, the California redbud is just as colorful as
the better-known California poppy. Myriads of tiny flowers
cloak the shrub's branches before the leaves
appear.

CARR CLIFTON

**B**attered but unbowed, ▲
this foxtail pine clings to life in
the rocky soil of the high
Sierra. Needles are short and
remain on the branches for 10-
12 years giving them a bushy,
foxtail-like appearance.

◄ **Like all true firs, red fir**
cones grow in an upright
position attached to branches in
the upper part of the tree.
Because of a silver cast to its
needles, red fir is sometimes
called "silvertip."

17

# The High Country

Guarding the eastern boundary of Sequoia National Park is Mount Whitney, at 14,495 feet the highest point in the contiguous United States. Stretching north, south, and west from this point and covering almost 1,000 square miles is the fabled "high Sierra." Two national parks, Sequoia and Kings Canyon, protect this wilderness heritage forever. A rugged land, the parks' backcountry is a backpacker's paradise for no roads cross this portion of the Sierra. Access is possible by a network of trails maintained by the National Park Service. Each summer finds the 700 miles of trail filled with hikers enjoying the languid days and the rain-free, star-filled nights.

ED COOPER

ED COOPER

◀ **Pointing rocky fingers nearly** 13,000 feet skyward, peaks of the Great Western Divide dominate the view. Thousands of years ago, tongues of ice filled the steep valleys on the flanks of the divide. Now the divide splits runoff. East of the mountains waters flow to the Kern River. The Kaweah River captures water falling to the west of the peaks.

**"Rock on rock, ice on ice...." These words were** ▲ penned by Col. John C. Fremont during his crossing of the southern Sierra nearly 150 years ago. Nothing has changed!

**John Muir said, "Going to the** ▷ mountains is going home." Thousands of hikers do just that every year. Warm summer temperatures, white fluffy clouds, and infrequent thunderstorms spell joy for the Sierran backpacker.

PAT O'HARA—DRK PHOTO

◀ **A craggy peak in Kings Canyon** National Park is reflected in one of the many lakes that dot the backcountry. Dominated by rock and snow, stunted pines reflect the harsh conditions of life in the high mountains.

# Lakes and Rivers

GARY LADD

DAVID MUENCH

△ **M**t. Clarence King glows as the last rays of the setting sun light up its rocky summit. Mirror-like, one of the many lakes in Sixty Lake Basin reflects its golden image with extraordinary clarity.

**T**he rushing water of Roaring River ▷ Falls leaps from its rocky cleft and in a white sheet of foam plunges into the basin below. Easily accessible, this scenic gem is but 200 yards from the main road in Cedar Grove.

△ **T**he clear, cold waters of Evolution Creek, in Kings Canyon National Park, beckon to the thirsty traveler. Nectar of the gods? Not anymore! A microscopic organism (Giardia lamblia) is found in most backcountry water supplies and can infect man. So, although the water looks pure and inviting, drink it only after filtering or boiling.

## Life in the High Country

The land of snow and ice—the Arctic—lies 3,000 miles north of the Sierra Nevada. Yet, here in these mountains at elevations above 10,000 feet, living conditions are remarkably similar. Temperatures during the winter drop well below zero and seldom rise above freezing. A deep mantle of snow blankets all but the windswept peaks. Summers are short and frost is not uncommon. Such a harsh environment allows only a few specially-adapted plants and animals to survive.

PAT O'HARA

*A hiker along the Pacific Crest trail ▷ crosses the high, rocky flanks of the Black Giant in northern Kings Canyon. The harsh climate prevents the growth of most vegetation.*

▽ *To find the sky pilot, climb the highest mountains, for this flower grows only in the shallow, sandy soils of true alpine country. At such high elevations, 11,000-14,000 feet, the sky becomes purplish much like the color of the sky pilot.*

ED COOPER

PAT O'HARA

▲ *Shooting stars are common throughout the parks. One variety grows as low as 1,200 feet. Most species prefer moist locales.*

GARY LADD

△ **P**ussy paws is abundant throughout the parks. A close look reveals dense, overlapping flower clusters which resemble the paws of a cat. Chipmunks relish the tiny black seeds.

**C**alifornia mule deer are ▷ native to both parks. Some live in the foothills the year-round, although most move to higher elevations as spring advances up the mountainsides. With the first heavy snow, the deer retreat to the foothills to spend the winter.

STEPHEN J. KRASEMANN—DRK PHOTO

◁ **T**he cony, pika, or rock rabbit lives a solitary life amid the talus slopes and rock slides of the high mountains. Midday hikers often hear its nasal-like bleat and by careful searching may see one perched on a rock, alert for danger.

**O**verleaf: Highest of ▷ them all, Mt. Whitney crowns the Sierra Nevada. Photo by Ed Cooper.

23

First Auto in Sequoia National Park owned by H. Hays. June 11, '10

◄ *Sequoia* National Park entered the automobile age in 1904 when the first auto reached Giant Forest. As roads improved, traffic increased— and during 1988, over 660,000 vehicles used park roads.

◄ **In 1886, the Kaweah Cooperative** Commonwealth of California began construction of a logging road to its claims in Giant Forest. The road was completed in 1890, but all claims were ruled invalid. Not a single giant was cut.

## Early History at Sequoia and General Grant National Parks

Although the parks were established in 1890, the public made little use of them at first. Access was difficult and visitor facilities were lacking. The first road into the park, begun by the Kaweah colonists, was completed to Giant Forest by the U.S. Army in 1903. The next year the first auto arrived at Giant Forest where a tent camp supplied meals and beds to adventurous travelers. At General Grant National Park, similar facilities opened. Not until 1935 did the Generals Highway link the two parks.

NPS PHOTO

▲ **The giant trees most** likely were named for the noted Cherokee Indian scholar and leader Sequoyah. This talented man recorded the Cherokee language and is honored in Statuary Hall, Washington, D.C.

NPS PHOTO

▲ **Led by his** Potwisha Indian friends, Hale Tharp, a pioneer Three Rivers cattleman, "discovered" the Giant Forest in 1858.

◀ **The Civilian Conservation Corps or CCC** was responsible for much development here during the 1930s. At the height of its success, over 1,000 men were at work in 12 camps throughout the parks. Here they work on one of the many trails built during their stay.

NPS PHOTO

**Cutting the** ▷ Mark Twain tree took eight days of hard labor before it finally crashed to earth in 1891. A nearly perfect specimen, the basal section is still on display in the American Museum of Natural History. The stump's location in Grant Grove's Big Stump Basin is marked by an exhibit.

JEFF GNASS

## The Foothills

For average summer visitors, the Sierra foothills are nothing more than one final barrier to surmount before reaching their destination, the true mountains. Hot and appearing lifeless, the brown hillsides stand parched and desolate. However, with the wet season comes change. As though touched by a magician's wand, the sere landscape comes alive with the vibrant colors of life. The rich green of new grass, the fresh green leaves of the buckeye, and a kaleidoscope of millions of colorful flowers transform the barren hills and valleys into one vast garden. Animal activity also increases. The acorn woodpecker and the scrub jay now must share their domain with others of their kind. Ground squirrels emerge from their burrows. Even man begins to take a greater interest in the world around him. However, too soon the rains disappear. Too soon the long, hot days reappear. Too soon nature's colorful extravaganza moves on to higher places. And once again, the foothills don their cloak of brown to await the return of the magician.

▲ **G**reen—the color of money, but also the color of life! The soaking rains of winter and spring are responsible for the lush vegetation bordering this rocky cascade. But here the rains end in April, and the searing heat of summer will soon change the green to brown. The stream will cease to flow and simply become another of the countless foothill arroyos.

**T**his tall inhabitant of the foothills, ▷ Ithuriel's spear, is very common on grassy slopes, growing up to a foot and a half high. It blooms in April and is one of six species all known as Indian potato. Indians ate the bulb of the plant, either raw or roasted. It tastes much like the Irish potato.

PAT O'HARA—DRK PHOTO

GERRY REYNOLDS

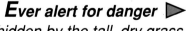 **High in the**
mountains within Sequoia
National Park, snow still
covers the peaks of the
Sierra. Storing the melt
from these snowy bastions,
Lake Kaweah, outside the
park, glistens amid the
spring greenery.

*Ever alert for danger* ▷
*hidden by the tall, dry grass,*
*two mule deer search for the*
*cause of alarm. Although*
*protected within the national*
*parks from man, the deer*
*remain subject to the predator/*
*prey relationships that govern*
*the lives of wild animals*
*everywhere.*

JOHN J. PALMER

▲ **In summer, the clear, sweet song** of the hermit thrush is heard throughout Sierran forests. Winters are spent in the foothills below the snow.

PHILLIP D. NORDIN

▲ **Butterflies are most abundant in the** tropics, although about 700 species are found in North America north of Mexico. Boisduval's blue is one of several blues found throughout the parks.

LARRY NORRIS

◀ **Mirroring the blue of Sierran skies,** the bowl-shaped flowers of baby blue eyes are found in moist meadows of the foothills, blooming from February to May.

JOHN J. PALMER

◀ **Moths rest** during daylight hiding their underwings. The rosy underwing's true glory can only be seen when it spreads its wings.

LARRY NORRIS

**Harlequin lupine is one of a number of lupines** ▶ found in the foothills. Its multicolored flower makes it easy to distinguish from numerous purplish lupines.

CHUCK PLACE

△ **In the foothills, the yellow** blooms of the fiddleneck are the first to shout "Spring!"

**Just a glimpse** ▷ of its rust-red tail is sufficient to identify the adult red-tailed hawk. Ground squirrels, mice, snakes, and lizards are its chief food items.

HERBERT CLARKE

JOSEF MUENCH

△ **Like many foothill plants, the California buckeye has developed special** adaptations to allow it to flourish in arid situations. The buckeye leafs out in late winter, acquires large, showy clusters of white flowers in May, and drops its leaves in midsummer. By September, only pear-shaped seed pods remain hanging from the tips of its leafless branches.

# *Kings Canyon Route to Cedar Grove*

Kings Canyon National Park is made up of two sections. The main section is wilderness, more than 450,000 glorious acres. Sticking out like an undersized thumb from the mass of Sequoia National Park is the other part, the Grant Grove area. The Nation's Christmas Tree is found here as well as the largest of all remaining sequoia groves, Redwood Mountain. From Grant Grove, a spectacular road leads 30 miles to Cedar Grove and the actual Kings Canyon. Leaving the forests of Grant Grove, the road begins a steep descent through cutover remnants of once-mighty sequoias till suddenly, a vast panorama appears. Here, on a grand scale, are the canyons of the mighty El Rio de los Santos Reyes, the Kings River. The road, dropping steeply, enters the granite-walled inner canyon of the South Fork. At first narrow and V-shaped, the character of the canyon upriver changes to a broad U-shaped valley. Here, on the banks of the river, is Cedar Grove.

GARY LADD

◄ **Moisture-**laden air cools as it rises and loses its ability to hold water. Water vapor condenses into fine particles of water, producing clouds at higher elevations or fog near the ground. Misty scenes like this are common during spring and fall.

**Kings Canyon** ▷ near Cedar Grove strongly resembles Yosemite Valley. Carved by the slow movement of glacial ice thousands of years ago, the valley exhibits all of the features of Yosemite to the north but on a smaller scale.

# At Cedar Grove

▲ **High on the canyon wall, the Sphinx** catches the early morning light. With the glaciers' disappearance, the small canyon to the left of the Sphinx now serves as an avalanche chute.

◀ **With its feet** almost in water, the yucca or Spanish bayonet is living dangerously. High water in the Kings River is notorious for its volume and swiftness.

▲ **The reddish-brown, deeply-**furrowed bark and the fragrant wood help to identify this tree as incense cedar, for which Cedar Grove was named. Fire, which did not harm the tree, caused the black char on the trunk.

ED COOPER

JEFF GNASS

▲ **Meadows are as** much a part of the Sierra scene as Big Trees and mountains. And meadows too undergo a slow, gradual change. As trees encroach on Zumwalt Meadow in Kings Canyon, the meadow will eventually disappear to be replaced by a forest of yellow pine.

**Revealing its icy** ▷ origin, the characteristic U shape of Kings Canyon stands outlined in the afternoon haze. Glacial ice, more than 2,000 feet thick, scraped and tore at the hard granite, eventually carving the canyon into its present form.

# Mineral King

On a hot summer day, the fragrance of pine mingling with a cool, mountain breeze is true treasure for anyone lucky enough to be in Mineral King. But the valley first attracted attention in the 1870s for a different kind of treasure—silver. Although the bonanza was found only in prospectors' imaginations, it caused the construction of a twisting, 25-mile road opening up the valley. For the next 85 years, Mineral King remained a simple, summer-cabin community. Attracting the attention of downhill skiers in the sixties, it soon became the focus of controversy between developers and environmentalists. Congress settled the issue in 1978 by making it part of Sequoia National Park.

PHILLIP D. NORDIN

▲ **Butterflies fly by day** and rest with their wings erect. A good photographer needs patience and skill.

◄ **For automobiles, the** road ends in Mineral King valley. For hikers, the trails begin there. One explores the canyon and lake country to the west, including the Hockett Plateau. Another heads south to the Kern Canyon over 11,680-foot Franklin Pass. The third goes north over Timber Gap, where it joins a network of other backcountry trails.

GERRY REYNOLDS

GERRY REYNOLDS

GERRY REYNOLDS

▲ *The colorful* mountains that surround Mineral King rise quickly. Highest of them all is Sawtooth Peak, elevation 12,343 feet. When viewed from a distance, the sawtooth portion is unmistakable.

◄ *The road to Mineral* King closes with the first heavy snow of winter. Except for an infrequent skier or a patrol ranger, the valley is quiet. Only the roar of winter storms disturbs the snowbound silence.

GARY LADD

▲ **The late afternoon sun glistens on polished** *granite. Thousands of years ago, the same sun glistened not on rock but on ice. Dusy Basin was the home of a glacier. Like a giant piece of sandpaper the glacier, moving slowly over the unyielding granite, ground and polished it to a high sheen. Warming temperatures spelled doom for the glaciers, and most disappeared about 10,000 years ago.*

## The Parks in Transition

Every year, over 2,000,000 people visit Sequoia and Kings Canyon National Parks. Every year, over 660,000 vehicles travel the parks' 120 miles of paved road. And every year, the same problems that plague the nation increase—overcrowding, air pollution, water pollution, and crime. Answers to these problems are complex and, in many instances, not yet available. Nevertheless, steps to counteract these threats must be taken soon. Perhaps in the not too distant future, heavily-visited parks will limit the number of park visitors. Length of stay may be adjusted. Whatever the remedy, it will be done with only one thought in mind, to protect and preserve for the enjoyment of future generations. Already, backcountry use in Sequoia and Kings Canyon is regulated by permit. Will the frontcountry be next?

LARRY ULRICH

◄ **Few park visitors** *realize the treasures that lie beneath their feet as they tour the parks. But spelunkers know that the parks protect over 80 caves. They occur in marble, a few are quite large, and some are highly decorated. One of the best is Crystal Cave. It is open to the public and tours are given daily during the summer months. The cave is managed by the Sequoia Natural History Association under contract to the National Park Service.*

**A**bove tree line in Evolution ◭
Basin in Kings Canyon National
Park, a lone hiker makes his way
along the heavily-traveled John Muir
trail. Completed in 1932, the trail
quickly became extremely popular.
During the last 20 years, relocation
of the route out of meadows and
other delicate places has done much
to lessen the impact on fragile
backcountry resources.

◁ **P**eeking from behind a tree, this
black bear appears to be playing hide and
seek. But, please, don't join in the fun. Keep
your distance and remember that no matter
how cute they seem to be, bears remain
wild, powerful animals. Getting too close
could result in a serious injury to you and
perhaps death to the bear.

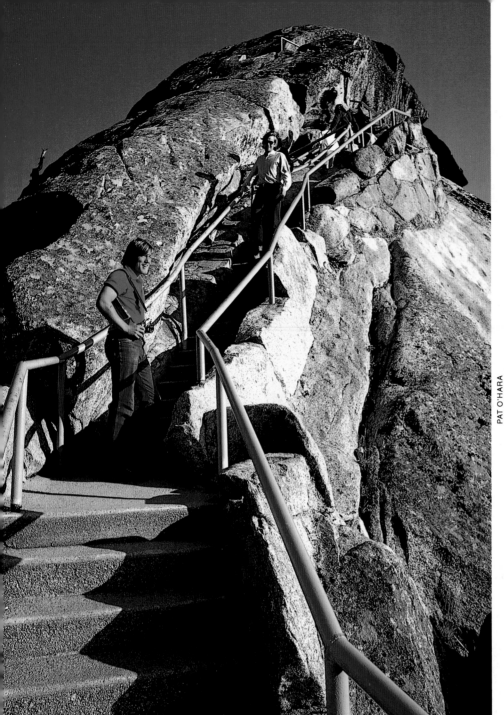

PAT O'HARA

# Parks Mean Different Things to Different People

RICHARD C. BURNS

▲ **All things are protected in** national parks. This young person is acting correctly, looking but not touching. Most wild creatures are perfectly capable of looking after themselves and do not need our help.

◄ **Since the first steps were built in** 1917, Moro Rock has been a special attraction for park visitors. Today, steps and stout railings allow even the most timid to climb to the top of this huge monolith for a grand view of the Great Western Divide and the Kaweah River canyon.

**Many backpackers** ▷ carry fishing gear into the backcountry, and for good reason. Hungry trout abound in the lakes and streams. Even the novice fisherman can taste the results of his efforts at suppertime.

PAT O'HARA

GERRY REYNOLDS

◀ **During the summer months,** the Pear Lake cabin is a ranger's home. During the winter, it's home to numerous cross-country skiers. The Sequoia Natural History Association operates the hut and charges a modest fee for its use. Complete with 10 bunks, wood pellet stove, and plenty of snow, the hut is 6.5 steep miles from Wolverton. Reservations are required.

**How long has it been** ▼ since you gathered around a campfire, roasted hot dogs, and exercised your vocal cords on the "oldies but goodies"? This scene at Sunset Rock occurs several times a summer when visitors join park interpreters for a good old-fashioned songfest.

41

# Park Research in the Field and Behind the Scenes

▲ **P**ark research helps provide answers to resource problems. Here, using a radio tracking device, *scientists learn more about bears. A small radio transmitter, installed in a collar, is placed around the animal's neck. A portable antenna tracks the animal by receiving an audible signal from the transmitter. From such studies we have learned that relocating problem bears from heavily-used frontcountry areas to remote backcountry sites is counterproductive. Bears quickly return to their old territory, and an expensive helicopter ride is wasted. Current efforts are directed toward depriving bears of human food.*

◄ **T**he great age of *giant sequoias has intrigued scientists ever since the species was discovered. Because growing conditions are reflected in a tree's growth rings, researchers are using the rings to establish a calendar of climates extending back several thousand years. Naturally, their work is restricted to those giant sequoias cut before park protection.*

▲ **S**imple cabins for simple times—or at least they appear that way to us. Some ▲ notched logs, handsplit shakes for a roof, and the job was done. The Squatters cabin (above left) was built in 1886 by John Vest, a member of the socialist Kaweah Colony. Learning later that the property belonged to Hale Tharp, the first Caucasian settler in Giant Forest, Vest abandoned his cabin and never returned. Tharp's summer dwelling was unequaled in design! Using a hollow sequoia, a few boards, and some rocks for a chimney, he created a unique summer home. John Muir called the place "a noble den." Both cabins are maintained by the National Park Service as reminders of the park's history.

◁ **O**ne of the greatest threats facing Sequoia and Kings Canyon National Parks is the deterioration in air quality. Not only do pollutants reduce visibility (climb Moro Rock and see for yourself), but they also affect whole ecosystems. A program has been established to measure air pollution and also to determine its effects on park resources. Preliminary results show that park forests are indeed suffering from polluted air. These same studies also show that most of the pollution is generated outside the parks and transported to them by prevailing winds. Will society act before the results are irreversible?

◀ **Most park** trails are steep, rocky, and too difficult for use by the disabled. So, using donated funds, volunteers helped construct the Trail For All People. Located in the Giant Forest, the trail is smooth and level for wheelchairs. Exhibits tell the story of meadow and forest. Everyone, regardless of disability, can now experience firsthand the majesty of the giant trees.

NPS PHOTO

## SUGGESTED READING

ARNO, STEPHEN. *Discovering Sierra Trees*. Yosemite and Sequoia national parks: Yosemite and Sequoia natural history associations, 1973.

BASEY, HAROLD. *Discovering Sierra Reptiles and Amphibians*. Yosemite and Sequoia national parks: Yosemite and Sequoia natural history associations, 1976.

BEEDY, EDWARD C., and STEPHEN L. GRANHOLM. *Discovering Sierra Birds*. Yosemite and Sequoia national parks: Yosemite and Sequoia natural history associations, 1985.

DILSAVER, LARY M. and WILLIAM C. TWEED. *Challenge of the Big Trees: A Resource History of Sequoia and Kings Canyon National Parks*. Sequoia National Park, California: Sequoia Natural History Association, 1990.

GRATER, RUSSELL K. *Discovering Sierra Mammals*. Yosemite and Sequoia national parks: Yosemite and Sequoia natural history associations, 1978.

HARVEY, H. T.; H. S. SHELLHAMMER; and R. E. STECKER. *The Giant Sequoia*. Sequoia National Park: Sequoia Natural History Association, 1980.

HILL, MARY. *Geology of the Sierra Nevada*. Berkeley: University of California Press, 1975.

TWEED, WILLIAM C. *Sequoia & Kings Canyon: The Story Behind the Scenery*. Las Vegas, Nevada: KC Publications, Inc., 1997.

## *Sequoia Natural History Association*

The Sequoia Natural History Association (SNHA) was founded in 1940 to aid and promote scientific research and educational activities in Sequoia and Kings Canyon National Parks. As a nonprofit organization, SNHA makes a wide variety of publications available by mail and at park visitor centers. Guided tours of Crystal Cave are given daily during the summer months by SNHA staff. For more information, contact SNHA: HCR 89 Box 10, Three Rivers, CA 93271; (209) 565-3759; or on the internet: home page <http://www.nps.gov/seki/snha/htm>.

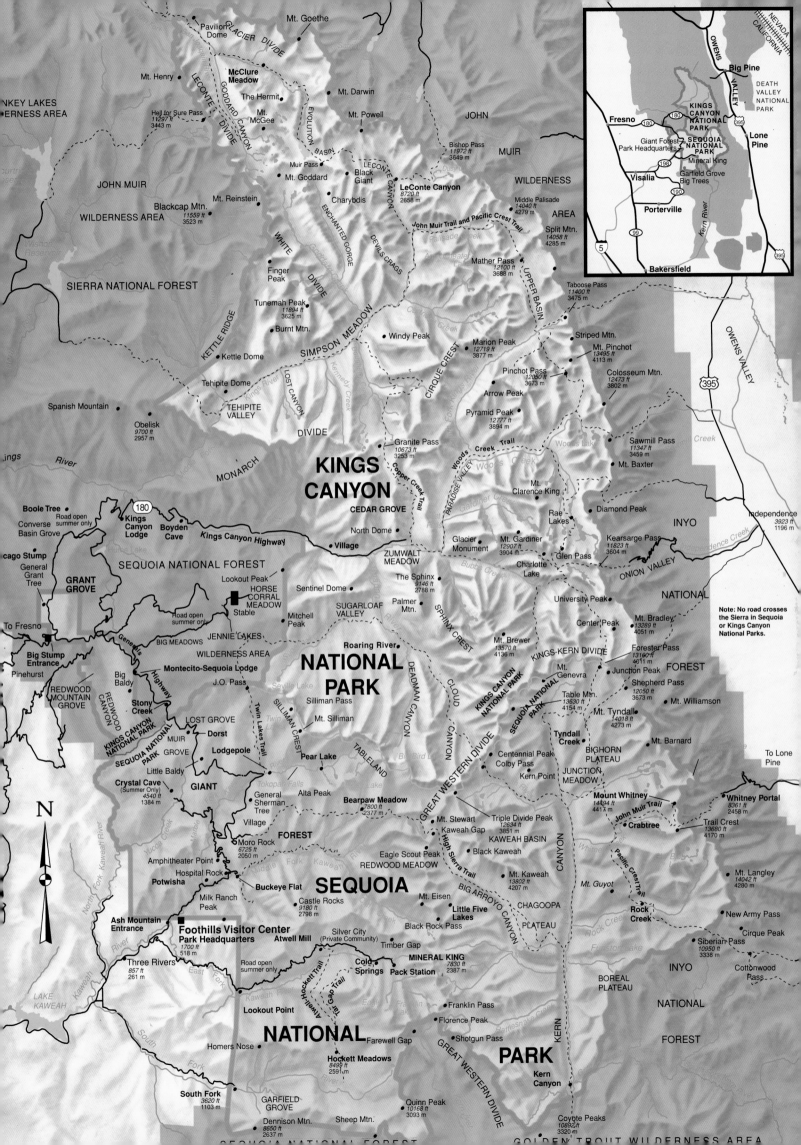

More than a century has passed since John Muir explored the fragrant forests, lush meadows and sun-drenched high country of Sequoia and Kings Canyon National Parks. Since that time, California has changed irreversibly and the results of twentieth-century life are everywhere. But the parks remain, islands in a sea of change. The towering red giants continue to be "first to catch the morning light, last to kiss the sun good night." The massive bulk of Mount Whitney continues to defend Sequoia's eastern approaches despite the thousands of people who climb its rocky limbs and successfully reach its windswept summit. And bear, deer, and countless other organisms continue to live out their lives according to nature's age-old rhythms. So long as these two magnificent parks exist, man too can continue to find food for his soul and balm for his spirit.

DICK DIETRICH

*The Senate Group of giant sequoias is found along the Congress trail in Giant Forest.*

LARRY ULRICH

▲ **In its lifetime, a single sequoia will produce enough seeds for 60 million** offspring. Yet only a few will germinate and fewer still grow to maturity. Perhaps one of the fortunate few, this tiny seedling has begun an existence that may extend over 3,000 years.

**Inside back cover:** Fog ▷ is a welcome companion of the General Sherman tree. Photo by Chuck Place.

**Back cover:** Bullfrog ▷ Lake shimmeringly reflects West Vidette and Deerhorn Mountain. Photo by Carr Clifton.

**Books in this "*in pictures ... The Continuing Story*" series are:** Arches & Canyonlands, Bryce Canyon, Crater Lake, Death Valley, Everglades, Glacier, Glen Canyon-Lake Powell, Grand Canyon, Grand Teton, Hawai`i Volcanoes, Mount Rainier, Mount St. Helens, Olympic, Petrified Forest, Rocky Mountain, Sequoia & Kings Canyon, Yellowstone, Yosemite, Zion.

**Translation Packages are also available.** Each title can be ordered with a booklet in German, French, or Japanese bound into the center of the English book. Selected titles in both this series and our other books are available in up to 8 languages.

**The original National Park series,** "The Story Behind the Scenery," covers over 75 parks and related areas. Other series include one on **Indian culture,** and the **"Voyage of Discovery"** series on the expansion of the western United States. To receive our catalog with over 110 titles:

**Call (800-626-9673), fax (702-433-3420), or write to the address below.**

*Published by KC Publications, 3245 E. Patrick Ln., Suite A, Las Vegas, NV 89120.*

***Created, Designed, and Published in the U.S.A.***
Printed by Doosan Dong-A Co., Ltd., Seoul, Korea
Paper produced exclusively by Hankuk Paper Mfg. Co., Ltd.